Let's Read About...
George W. Bush

To my brother-in-law, Tarique
— S.F.

To Alexis and David Boeshaar, caring friends.
In remembrance of my parents,
William J. and Merlyn Heyer.
To all with love.
— C.H.

No part of this publication may be reproduced in whole or in part, or stored in a retrieval system, or transmitted in any form or by any means, electronic, mechanical, photocopying, recording, or otherwise, without written permission of the publisher. For information regarding permission, write to Scholastic Inc., Attention: Permissions Department, 557 Broadway, New York, NY 10012.

ISBN 0-439-45953-2

Text copyright © 2003 by Sonali Fry.
Illustrations copyright © 2003 by Carol Heyer.
All rights reserved. Published by Scholastic Inc.
SCHOLASTIC, CARTWHEEL BOOKS, SCHOLASTIC FIRST BIOGRAPHIES,
and associated logos are trademarks and/or registered trademarks of Scholastic Inc.

Library of Congress Cataloging-in-Publication Data available.

12 11 10 9 8 7 6 5 4 3 2 1   3 4 5 6 7 8/0

Printed in the U.S.A.
First printing, January 2003

Scholastic First Biographies

Let's Read About... George W. Bush

by Sonali Fry
Illustrated by Carol Heyer

SCHOLASTIC INC.
Cartwheel BOOKS
New York   Toronto   London   Auckland   Sydney
Mexico City   New Delhi   Hong Kong   Buenos Aires

George Walker Bush was born on July 6, 1946, in New Haven, Connecticut. His parents are named George Herbert Walker Bush and Barbara Bush.

George W. and his parents moved
to Texas when he was two.
George W. loved being a Texas cowboy!

The Bush family grew.
George W. soon had three brothers
and a sister.

There were many politicians
in George W.'s family.
But George W. did not want to be
a politician.
What did he want to be?

A major-league baseball player!
George W. loved baseball.
He had watched his father become
a baseball star in college.
Young George W. wanted to be a star, too!

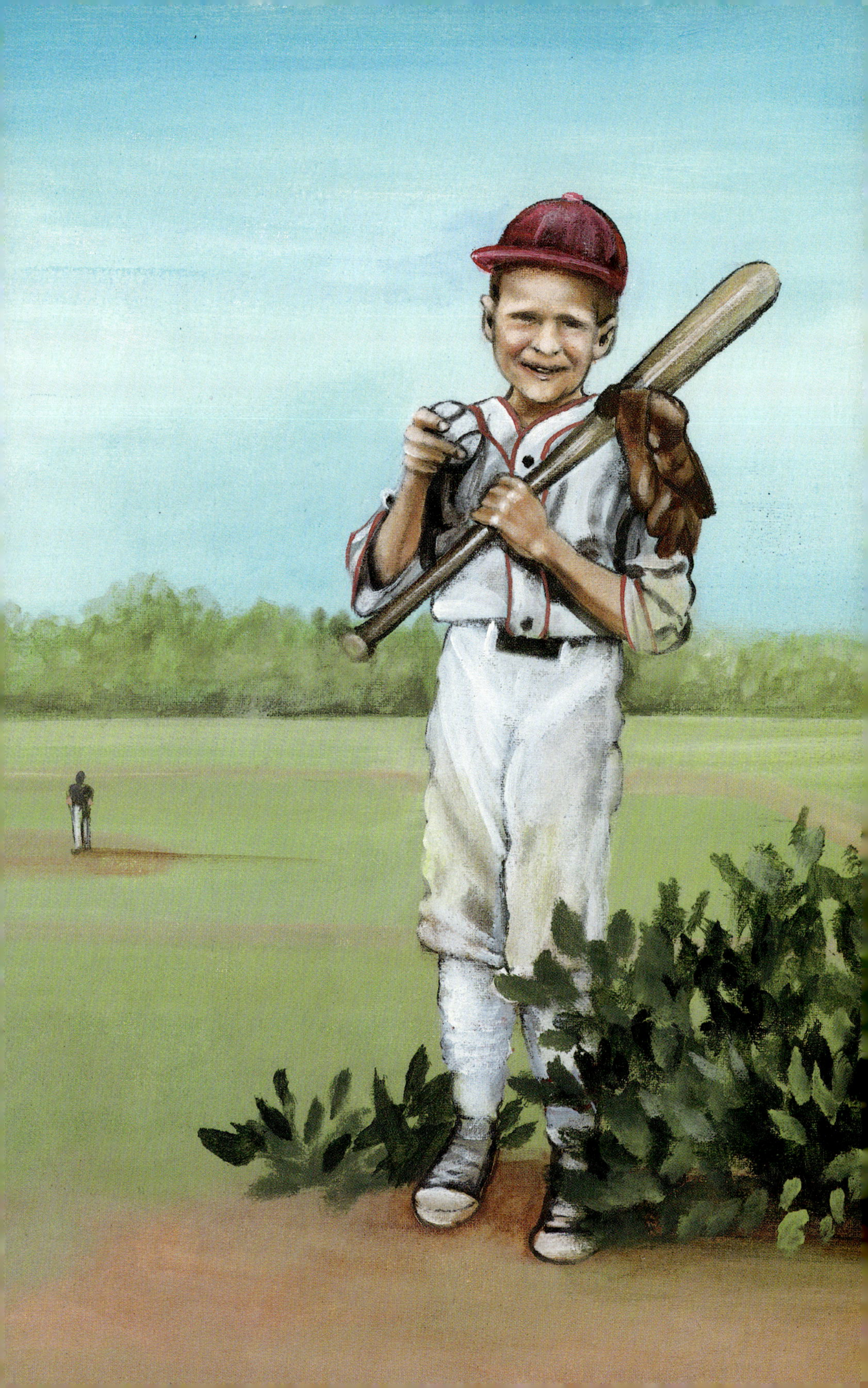

George W. was very friendly.
He always made people laugh!
He was the most popular boy in school.

George W. graduated from Yale University in 1968.
Then he joined the Texas National Guard.
He learned to be a fighter pilot.
George W. loved to fly planes.

George W. went to Houston a few years later.
There, he worked with boys who were very poor.

George W. loved this job.
He played games with the boys.
He even took them for airplane rides!

George W. went to Harvard Business School in 1973.
He did not know what he wanted to be.

George W. moved back to Texas
after he finished school.
He quickly found work in the oil business.
Soon, he started his own company.

George W. married Laura Welch in 1977. Laura was a librarian at an elementary school.
That year, George W. ran for Congress. Laura joined him on the campaign trail.

George W. lost the election in 1978.
But there were good times to come.
Laura Bush gave birth to twin girls
in 1981.

Then George W.'s father decided to run for president of the United States. George W. sold his oil business and moved his family to Washington, D.C.

George W. advised his father and wrote speeches for him.
He was thrilled when his father was elected president in 1988.

George W. still loved baseball.
He and some friends bought
the Texas Rangers baseball team.
George W. loved spending time
with the baseball players.

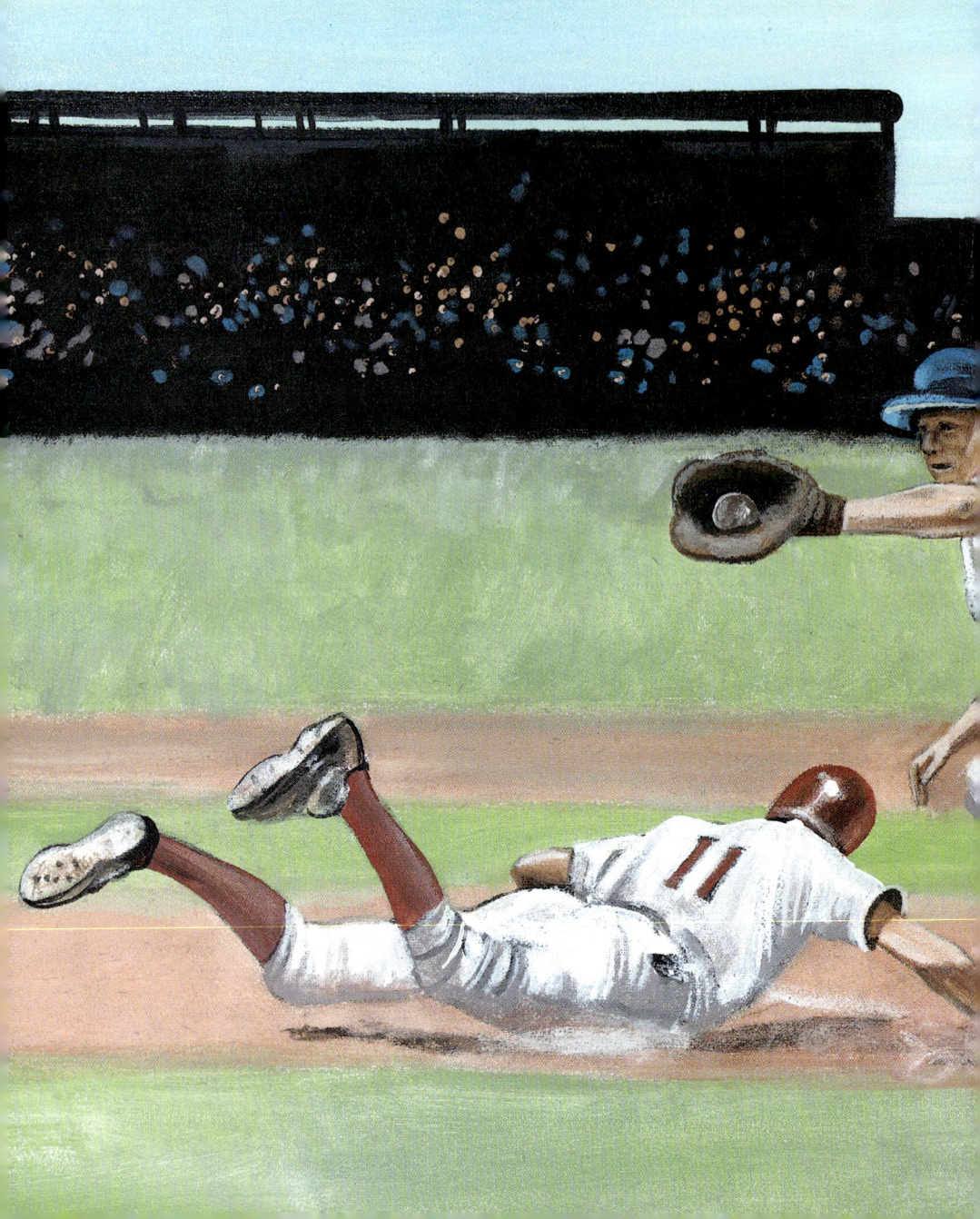

He knew the name of every person in the ballpark! He even had baseball cards with his picture printed on them!

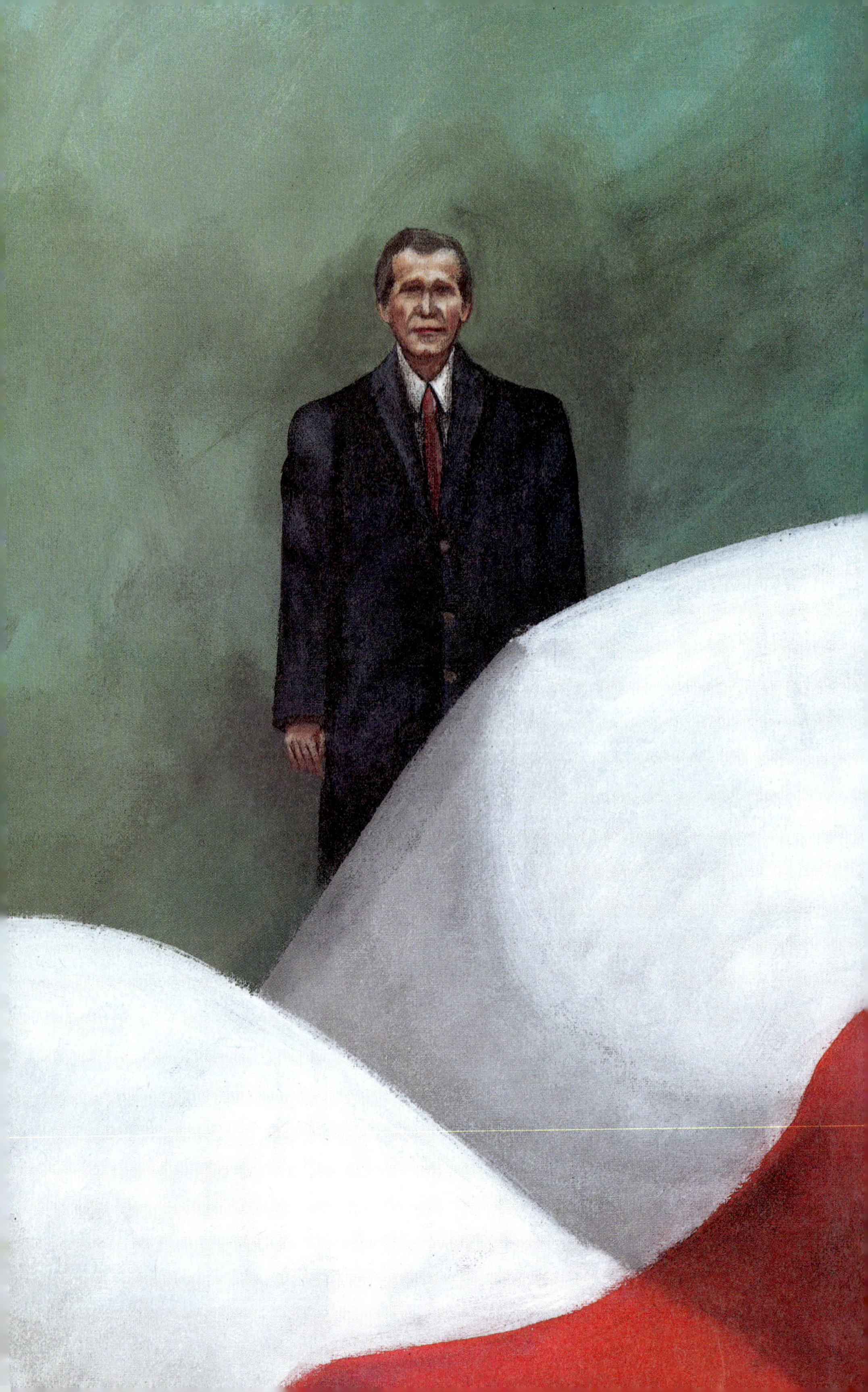

George W. ran for governor of Texas
a few years later.
George W. knew it would be a tough race.

George W. traveled all over Texas.
He spoke to as many people as he could.
George W. was cheerful and friendly.
People listened.

George W. won the election.
He became governor of Texas in 1994.

George W. was a good governor.
People liked him.

George W. ran for president in 2000.
Richard "Dick" Cheney was his running mate.
George W. belonged to the Republican Party.
Vice President Al Gore was his opponent.
Al Gore belonged to the Democratic Party.

Election night was very, very long.
It was a really close race.

There had to be a recount!
Finally, George W. won.

George W. Bush was sworn in as the forty-third president of the United States on January 21, 2001.

This was an historic moment. There was only one other time in American history when a father and his son had both been president. That was in 1825.

George Bush

George W. Bush

John Adams

John Quincy Adams

George W. promised to be
a good president.
He knew that it was going
to be a hard job.

George W. Bush pledged to make the United States a better, stronger nation.